THE DISTANT SOUND

Christmas
2020

Kevin,
A wonderful Book
of Poems enjoy,
Maggie

THE DISTANT SOUND

Poems

Eliot Schain

SIXTEEN RIVERS PRESS

Published by Sixteen Rivers Press
P.O. Box 640663
San Francisco, CA 94164-0663
www.sixteenrivers.org

Library of Congress
Catalog Card Number: 2019947945
ISBN: 978-1-939639-22-6
Book design: Wayne Smith
Photography: Tim Goodman

ACKNOWLEDGMENTS

Poems previously published:

"The Disciple" *America, We Call Your Name, Poems of Resistance and Resilience* (Sixteen Rivers Press, 2017)

"Patio" *Miramar,* Number 3, 2015

"Where Were You" *fort da, The Journal of the Northern California Society for Psychoanalytic Psychology,* Spring 2012

"Softer" *Written Here, The Community of Writers Poetry Review,* 2016

"Tonic Minor" *Where Trees Give Way, Views from the Northwest Coast,* photographs by Tim Goodman, 2013

The author would like to thank Christopher Buckley, Daniel Halpern, Bruce Isaacson, Robert Hass, the Squaw Valley Community of Writers, the Napa Valley Writers Conference, and the members of Sixteen Rivers Press; with special thanks, posthumously, to Carolyn Kizer and Philip Levine.

FOR MARY

CONTENTS

I. FRIENDS

II. AS IF TO SAVE ME

III. GRACE

IV. ON THE FRONTIER

As all the Heavens were a Bell,
and Being, but an Ear...

—Emily Dickinson

I

FRIENDS

THE OLD SHEPHERD

When the sound took me out of the house and into the yard
it grew wings and en-colored like that lofty earth-bird
who will not flee us so I stayed close to the sound
and the nerve within that was always trembling
trembled again until I closed in on the ghosts
and their kind voices and empty forms so close to mine
like those cracks in the universe leaking still more color
until I could not *what we call see* but could feel and hear
so I followed the sound as if drinking from the chalice again
and continued through the city with its warrens and cafes
and old homes carved out of nothing   as is everything
and then moved on to the countryside where lakes became
eyes dotting the earth's skin to lure me deeper into sound.

PILOT

We followed that sudden friend to the strange house
with the warm party and you drank without eating

then began flying paper planes around the room while
giggling as if the idea of flight were what you might

have to reckon with alone and cockeyed for years . . .
eventually I dragged you into the yard and soon the

street and finally the fields where I tried to feed you
milkweed and small animals but you kept gazing at

the heavens and drinking as your body thinned so I
lay next to you and began counting the stars and that's

when God whispered in my ear we are all aliens and
you were right to try flight as the only way to get in.

SATORI

I wandered up and down the hall looking for open rooms
with open windows and pools to swim in and trails to follow
and food to eat that would change me and then came the rest
of my life with its carports and electrical wires and dens for
hunkering down in yet here I am again in that vernal hallway
looking for rooms and pools and trails but mostly windows to
lean from and smell the breeze that has been inside all along.

GOD AND CREEK

When Jon was eight and went to the creek shaded by cottonwoods
in a distant city on the American Plain he was flooded by the miracle

of going home as the dappled light and the toads near the water and
the depressions in the ground that welcomed his bare toes reminded

his bones—though they would last a long, long time—that what would
make him a man was in the sound that comes by night or in those soft

corners of the day when the claptrap and the frittering are left behind ...
he placed his palms to the surface of that drifting water and its church

came into him as it would forever onward—for what *is* maturation but
the swelling reverence for this home we were given by some odd divine

who chose us to be both urn and ashes and so Jon accepted his town and
pecked with the others at what we might become but always remembered

the water from which the toads and the cottonwoods and all our gods
build their beautiful echoes with gates so we can be both human and free.

SPARK

When the lightning came through the socket in the house
he went out onto the Great American Plain to confront his maker

and in the thick night air with only smatterings of rain but the deep
thunder that tickles bone he thought of the visions that have changed

the world—the brave if slightly stupid ones in the lightning storm
with hands splayed against the sky and the human voice daring to find

an equivalent sound and then he thought of the love available to all of us
like electricity in the wall of a house that sometimes comes unbidden.

SOUNDS OF DISTANT SINGING

When men wake to sun in the fields near Lincoln
the story of who came before is not one
but action as Conestogas creak through
the brain and endless becomes a noun.
We quest here in Endless
where peeling away layers of land
grows us into something vast.
We are reliable hardware
when the purpose of breath is to bloom.
Bodies may come and go through
these so-called days chiming
but the particulars are only wind.
When we intone the dream we are greater
than wind in the ruins of the old European mind.

THE MAN WHO LIVED NEXT DOOR

The man who lived next door was a mystery. When I was young we called him retarded, the adjective we used for everything we couldn't explain. *That's* retarded, *she's* retarded. He would wear galoshes when it rained, but the few times he spoke—about the damaged fence, or the ruffians who plagued the block one fall— he did not reveal an accent. My mother thought he'd been in the war. My father defended his right to privacy, as if the man were a secret part of him. My friends and I would steal in through the gate to peek eagerly into the window but there was rarely much to see: a cereal box left on the table, a TV with snow, the flannel shirt hung over a chair as if mending itself. The one time we did catch him he was standing in the middle of the kitchen touching his throat—he looked panic-stricken. Years later on a trip home my father told me casually that our neighbor had died. His maid had found him, cried as if he'd been a lover. My father didn't say that—about the lover; that was my addition; I had learned a few things in the world and had begun to dream of him. He filled the recesses of my brain the way water creeps in, or the way clouds obstruct the sun, and there is no quick or easy way to be bright.

STRAP

When Tom was ten and first moved to the South there were many thrilling new experiences like grits and ringworm and forests in the city but most memorable

was that black strap hanging from the barber's chair he was put in shortly after arriving which readied the gleaming single-edged blade as ominously as anything

he'd seen prior then the blade came to the rear of his neck to trim further and make the border as straight as a machine as if that would solve his problems but he fell for

it for the barber was avuncular and had a shiny bald pate and that smarmy paternal friendliness Tom had yet to realize is a cloak for shame plus the man relayed lewd

stories found in hidden magazines as the blade whipped across the strap then came to trim Tom deeper. Lo these many years later Tom suspects the barber would have

drawn blood had he known what kind of man Tom would become since the distinction between desire and the brain is like the gulf between the old and young; now with less

hair and more sin Tom has come to fear those men of the South lingering like sloths put on earth to remind us this life we've come to love could end in the nick of time.

AMOS

When I heard the story of the snake-handling pastor
who'd got bitten and died because he demanded to go home
where God was more likely to find him than in some hospital room
I thought of you exploring the universe prior to the seminary
and the faith you pressed into me as if I were a nurse receiving
tools or some body part mysteriously severed away;
the Lord does work mysteriously and thus many years later
I find the YouTube video of you exhorting potential followers
to surrender to your faith and greet strange circumstance
like the pretty women at a hoedown which is why I always
consorted with the devil whenever I saw the tears in your eyes
those revisions you were given as a substitute for lonely
and lonely is what I smell now in the voice coming from the screen
so chipper and convincing most of all yourself that the answers
you were seeking have come like Adam to tame the snake.

PLATE

We visited John Brown's cave in the mid-sixties in southern Nebraska
where the land still reeked of our pioneer efforts to get to the other side

and the cave was sufficiently gloomy for there were still those race wars
raging far away in Kansas and LA and Newark and Birmingham triggered

by yet another twist on the dark and after we had toured it we came out into
the blinding light of another Great Plains day with its outdoor gift shop where

kind women were selling Kennedy memorabilia faster than anything about
that grim-visaged puritanical man who gave his life up for a violence warped

by the noble cause and so being of an impressionable age plus always on the
lookout for new heroes I used my allowance to buy a plate with the bright face

of our recently murdered president for I knew little about this country erupting
like the boils on Brown's face and naturally during the long drive home across

the empty plain I grew more enamored with my new hero as I traced the raw
ceramic edges and let a chewed thumbnail touch down on the strong brow

and cheekbones as if they might nourish me into the future but when we
finally arrived at the long white ranch house in a suburban part of Nebraska's

only real city where there were no black faces save the friendly domestics
bussed over to us I stepped from the back seat of our brand-new Chevrolet

and the plate slipped from my hands and broke into pieces against the hard
macadam that drapes the earth with more sin given to turn us into grim

gophers popping up for light after the rain or crusty lizards under the rocks
amid some weird inward kind of storm; I write this having been a lizard all

my life but when I hear about the men of Kansas and LA and Ferguson again
I taste the yoke of the hide-bound strap that steers our dark and nervous sons.

WHY WE DRINK

What I remember is we were wasted in the back of a Ford Fairlane
and Randy was speeding through the streets of Youngstown, Ohio . . .
he'd gotten both laid and laid off that day, a figurehead on the prow
of the ship of state going down. He was *crazy-drunk* too, so when
the sirens began, he yelled *hold on!* then took the back streets with
the kind of abandon I'd just encountered in that other horror movie
come to life—I was still on probation, you were the daughter of my
third stepfather and the force of our careening off the curbs as Randy
proved himself drove your body but not your brain into mine . . . and
best of all, we felt like we were still employed, so there was nothing
that fall evening could have poured us that wouldn't have tasted good.

THE DISCIPLE

He lifts the Cadillac up onto 80 going west
pulls a cigarette from the breast pocket of his denim shirt
though as a practicing Muslim he does not smoke
but the road is an addiction the Koran does not forbid
and the jobs he's quit and the books he's read were kindling
so now the flames inside burn no color and no religion
just one man trying to escape his plight via the promise
here on the fading yet still fecund stones of home.

THE NOVITIATES

All night long we tried to find it, he and I,
in that city on the edge, and in the wilderness,
which kept popping up through the cracks like church doors,
but nothing opened wide enough to let our bloated bodies in,
so we had to content ourselves with drinking and smoking
—whatever we could get down the pipes—and when our legs
began to give, we got back on the motorcycles and gunned
them over the bridge at speeds that made our armor shudder,
but we wouldn't die, and when we returned to earth, and eased
back into home, there was no roof this time, just fervent stars
behind distant clouds, waiting for the flames within to dim.

THE NEIGHBORHOOD

I still recall the truck stop outside Bakersfield,
where the filthy mirror in the men's room
tried to slow me down
but all I could see were those sad and honest eyes,
the ones that wrote my Bible,
so I drew wet fingers down my cheeks
and pinched the throat, and whispered *yes*,
the way Lewis did, and Walt and Jack,
and all the rest I'd driven into my companions
in that Mustang stolen from the shed of heaven,
for vast was all we needed;
but when I look into mirrors now
the eyes are not so kind—so many friends are gone,
and the neighborhood is shrinking back
through infant mind to memory, though if I touch the
glass the way I once touched my throat,
the world and all its catalysts can sometimes come again.

ANOTHER GIFT

We drove the hitchhiker down the dirt road to the cabin in the middle of the apple farm; it was Christmas eve and raining; everything exuded that Washington mist so we took it inside thinking our philosophy of serendipity would bless the hitchhiker and his family and the potbelly stove they used for heat; there were a few presents wrapped and the wife, who was pregnant with another, looked strained when our newly found friend asked if we could spend the night—it was as if Jesus had grown deformed, so my partner and I slept in the barn, where the apples had rolled in, for the folly of man is the gifts we are given when a dark night hitches its way to dawn.

TRANSIT

Jim boards the long-distance bus to avoid doing further damage
and takes a window seat next to the dark woman who
keeps swatting at her child from across the aisle.
He looks out at the passing factories, the fields
as their tussling continues, for there is no surcease on the earth.
Yet somewhere between this emptiness and a resurrected heaven,
the beating ceases and the blacktop beneath them
pulls up the ghosts, and now the bus runs smoothly,
like that other place waiting, where forgiveness makes us different.

THE WILDS

My friend and I would ride our bikes up the long winding canyon road
to the Neutra house on the edge of Coyoteland where he lived with

an Israeli mom and Midwestern dad and then we'd pedal wisely on
huffing and laughing at the way our lungs took us to the edge of extinction

before we'd return to collapse in his driveway and glide our arms and
soiled hands toward the clear glass panels that shielded a bucolic atrium

and scarlet door from the mystery winds as if on the portico of paradise
but we wouldn't die and when the old quiet breath came back and his sad

home lit up with wild 45s and clever appliances relegating us to the thrill
of being still thirteen and bored quickly by everything we prayed night

would become the sole howl of animals and its dark sky would consume
our beauty then forge that wilder body before Earth would choose to rest.

II

AS IF TO SAVE ME

AMY AND SYLVIA

In a large lake house outside of Vergennes Vermont Amy began *The Bell Jar* and could not put it down and soon uncontrollably went out into the autumn air still

reading and slipped into the wood that ringed the shore and as her syntax began to fail and the caves hollowed out in Amy's mind all her clothes came off and she

muscled into formlessness and then oblivion for the deep grief such girls have left keeps emptying into the ancient lake as new bodies take in the gray wingless birds

that continue to fly into those cracks between what is known and wisely unknown to become wands of the nightmare and now the tar passing for hands bubbled up

and the One Who Made Us took Amy back into his creation and sent his darkest birds sliding through the trees like a birthmark which spreads until pigment is no

longer error and the blackened hearts ring in the bell jar for they sound like our emptiness as the foul circus heaves its most celebrated acts into the air for love.

THE GIRLS

Me and Elizabeth hiked up into Little Yosemite Valley before we could rightly read, so would mimic like starlings until every step, stone by stone, widened our paws … increased the mountain's sound, but after setting up our tent, awakened as women can be into its wondrous heat, we succumbed again to the human forms and began to rely on the savages within, though we soon learned horrid words for them, right syntax, and how passions in our country's lofty Coliseum can go awkwardly wrong.

WE ARE KING

From the window I watch you on all fours surveying the dirt in the garden
though the land is a mirage and you are remembering as I am remembering

which suggests the past which the Buddhists say is just mirage and reason
why the heart's the only organ that's not in it as you're in your false garden

pulling strays and planting seeds the way you did raising that boy in me . . .
oh lost mother who makes it so hard to love for the touch of skin is frost on

the window building the willow which ushers the divine down in costume . . .
and to pollute with your ardent heart is what we sweet sons guard against

as the mare rides down the sands then veers into the ocean where one thing
becomes another until we can finally live in the world . . . I fall apart with you

in mind and wander this big garden with the budding wand you hung over
the bed without warning since every majestic bloom is a woman un-weaned

and each castle has its crow flying within like your entranced eyes lingering.

PATIO

Your patio was for parties, a cement slab with a corrugated pea-green
roof, later embellished with Sears bar and grill, stereophonic sound,

mutable track lighting, and surrounded on three sides by blooming
jacaranda and bougainvillea, for this was post-war Los Angeles,

and the patios were stepping out, flushed with money and liquor,
the melodies of jazz, then British rock—a stage set for jaunty cravats

and diaphanous shirts that would look out over the lush, though not quite
Bel-Air space between a prosperous, but still working-class neighborhood

and the National Cemetery, where identical white tombstones stretched
like shuttered dominos with the cold, soulless efficiency your revelers

were trying to forget here on the patio—the price of one war paid,
another coming for painters, directors, shrinks and anesthesiologists ...

all immigrants bundled in victory amid the warm Mediterranean air,
where despite misalignments of marriage and career—the generalized

anguish that kept the depressants flowing—there was a sweetness to
this surcharged nation woven from yarns that crossed like rats on boats ...

affection in stray moments of this massive *quinceañera*, perfumed as it
was by the fumes of a nearby freeway and the balm of the hidden stars.

STILL BUILDING COUNTRY

In a backyard in Westchester the elm tree speckles with shadows
for today is our garden party and Emily in her newly pleated skirt

and well-known pig tails is trying in the way she's been trained to
give comfort to friends with lemonade and mint cookies for they

come from houses with "oodles" of money or at least it seems like
oodles to the old Jew in the city who's burned through his dreams

three times but still walks uptown with the sly violins in his head
and the eyes of the one daughter who knows what it is to be steel.

WHERE WERE YOU

I was in the second grade when Kennedy was shot
and Mrs. Siert, the epitome of sweet and pert with
bobbed hair and tightly tailored skirt put a hand
to her flushed face when the principal's voice came
over the intercom. She did not weep but changed
forever so we—just seven-year-olds busily falling
in love—had seven months to watch her become a
woman tinged with grief before launching into the
higher grades to find girls for us, while inside was
the altered feminine, which determines everything:
the duration of passion, the integrity of work . . . the
choice to march or not—redeem the fallen man or
become him, lay waste to our fragile lives and hers.

TENDER

In the small town of Delhi
pronounced Del-high
at the gas station on the corner
where Route 2 bends eastward
Bobby fills his tank then wanders
into the aisles of the mini-mart
to shadow a heavy-set
dull-eyed girl who must have
odd genes for there's
something in the way she shifts
yet still stares that suggests
these hills have been gnawing
at her kin since they came
one maybe two hundred years ago
when the Appalachians were
rubber bumpers before the Plains
and her kin lodged in because
sometimes dreams are pencil lines
on the wall the older sibling makes
and we feel forever under

he's only passing through
but if Bobby stayed he would slip into
the old hotel built for the river-men
and on loose springs and a damp mattress
dream again his escape from the body
which troubles the way weather can
—ominous then bright then ominous—
and draw closer to her sweaty neck
her eyes fixed on another bag of chips
to listen to her breathe.

SOFTER

When I read Rilke's eighth elegy
to the hunter I was doing business with
the trees stepped out of the forest
and mankind replaced them
while the animals
so often in his sights
examined each trunk eagerly
to consider what turn God had taken
as these new trees
or rather these new people
with their lingering brutalities
condemned their past
and their actions grew restrained
until a different story of man
flushed each trunk like a quick disease
leaving glyphs the animals
in their innocence could not read
and soon bright leaves began to fall
to bury the fascinated
transfixed bears and wolves
squirrels and circus stars
which you might think all died
but it was not the same kind of dying
as the mesh of decomposing fibers
let them breathe as they were going

my hunter relished what I was saying
for he had children and loved them
ate the deer he shot and loved them
but now moved deeper into
the top of his brain

which soon became a canopy
that would not fail with the seasons
but transformed the times
the way serious can if it wants to
if we stop preening for dicks
those little minds.

HOW VERDA SAVED ME

After I'd violated you
your Aunt Verda in rural Pennsylvania
prayed for us both as she laid hands on
the letters you sent and took them to her
prayer circle where her friends began
to cry and fall shaking to the ground

then Verda rode four hundred miles
on a bus to where we were staying
like newlyweds in a flophouse motel

when she arrived the thunderstorms began
so was soaked when she entered our room
but came straight for us
and fastened her lips to mine as if to save me
as if to save herself
which is why I struggle with the word *violation*.

THE CAD

When Jay got the results and realized he was still viable
he walked out into the suburban streets and gasped then
bent over to weep before weaving down the sidewalk past
every shrunken castle as he tried to contain his happiness
so as not to get arrested but it was hard for after his hands
boxed the wind they settled at his groin to re-mystify the
body and when he moaned only one soul heard him from
inside her closing garage so he imagined her naked on a
table then went back to loving the world again and again.

THE JOYS OF SORROW

I was bartending at the Chez Paree on November 7th 1991
when suddenly a man walked in as grim as a Russian with

a map of Vietnam tattooed down his arm (flanked by rifles
still blazing) and placed a tensed hand to the polished pine

I drop our town's finest drinks on. He ordered shots of gin
and began to groan before they came so my regulars June

and Candy, Mickey and Darnell halted their chatter to inch
toward him as if a world were opening the way those vast

doors at the plant down on High Street open and out rolls
exactly what we need. Darnell was the first to get touched

as his own tatted skin sent bone up the neck of the man to
work his childhood and before that the wandering of stars

and Candy moved in too, unearthing a love she had buried
so I withdrew to lay the stylus down on new sounds of sin

for there's likely tomorrow and the rain in the parking lot
falls on cars that like jellied cells in our veins take us from

here to the oyster opening, which is the true work of God.

MASTERPIECE

I step into the Gallery 41 of the Uffizi Museum and there on the wall is
The Doni Tondo, that early Michelangelo-portal to our human hands

in the garden—silky colors folding like the drift of stars over *Madonna*
and Child, her suitor Joe behind, all three twisted round as if the beast

were undone ... she angelic and pure, old Joe paternal, yet sadly aware
as the child squirms with impudence in the credible way children are,

crying *I will not be restrained!*—a prophecy for him in instinct comes!
who gets that so right? via paint that goes past paint through flesh and

into some Platonic beam of it, while the stolas unto Mary swoon with
the lights of heaven: gold tilting toward mustard, gun-metal blue, pink

from the love organ that needs no skin, and those mesmerizing arms!
I stand slack-jawed, honey-bellied, and kinetic where it counts—soon

dream of a suppleness among such vivid soft the sky itself could fling
down an early grave; I leave the room to ponder—return three times,

for three were needed, as the portrait preyed on *when we know God—*
a sight for a peeping St. John and his classical, nude, half-done figures

in the frieze: the blessings of antiquity: of balance, poise and fortitude;
enduring revelations in the eyes of men ... the price we paid for leaving.

PRESS

Moses stays suspended

searching the curved ceiling
with eager fingers
for cracks to push our history through

the way he had fallen in love

with an elder then a girl then his people
and thus the best of us
which coos in the way-back like a stream

of feeling at the core of being

and when he finds the cracks
although the heft will not separate
an ancient light comes through

like peals of sound

which lets some of him escape
as we all can when kneeling
or with language

or through flights into memory

where the other side surrounds us
and falling in love
is no longer something we do.

III

GRACE

THE SOURCE

We would roam the campus while still pre-teens then gather in the bowling alley to buy food on our own and listen to the jukebox songs shed light on what was coming and when it came there was an inverted fountain near the music building where we would strip down on lazy summer days and bury ourselves behind the falling water which was closer to our baying hearts than we had ever been before and sometimes we'd kiss but mostly talk about school dramas and personal slights or food and how the Great Whittler was doing with each of us; the summer passed languidly this way though we also shopped for clothes and soon chose colleges and then scattered with many shreds still hanging but when I recall the fountain and our intent studies there I know it was the core of learning and how books and all that other stuff came to be.

STAR TREK

My friend Adam was a movie star's son so we'd party at his home,
not because his dad was there—he was often filming and far away,
but the odd man lingered, in the headshots above the balustrade
and in the oysters that came from a gold saucer in the fridge; it was
the *lift and separate* that let the mansion and our skin conjoin a hefty
two feet off the body, like fresh boats docked just offshore with goods
from other countries ... I remember Belinda Himmelblau halfway up the
grand staircase looking down as she called to me in that shrill barker's
voice trained by afternoon TV ... she wanted new kinds of love, or rather
simple proof that it was permissible for her body not to be a star so she
just hung there as we all went deeper into our fantasies ... as we pushed
earnestly into outer space, which was actually deeper and deeper water.

CHOKECHAIN

Because we drove the bejeweled snaking roads
of Bel Air and its canyons as
the anatomy of my friends and I began to stir ...
and because desire roots to birth,
there was no house grand enough,
no garden bold enough for *the boys* ...
so we rose to the high desert shrubs and views
of the city choking and ejecting, like the pale one
in bondage who knows what we do to feel.

CITY OF THE ANGELS

When the movie premieres came to our town the year the war dragged on we
would wander to them from the home my parents had turned into a courtroom

and my boyfriend and I sheepishly held hands as we passed the concrete squares
my girlfriend and I had carved with bold initials in front of the house of the famous

ophthalmologist who had killed his wife then we moved on to the gardens at the
edge of the university where I'd first received the touch of another inside my clothes

and though it was not my boyfriend's touch he got super excited when I relayed the
story while standing in the long line outside the Paramount Theater inside of which

the famous star kept hoisting her sexy body onto a crippled soldier to convince him
there is more to life than trauma and we made out quietly during the scene where

the star gently wipes the soldier's gooey chin then shoots him with yet another gun
which was so close to cleansing and so close to waste and nearly what growing up

felt like and what *life still feels like* for there are so many ancient wars inside the
body where frustration keeps carving fraudulent initials into quickly disappearing

streets but then again it's why people need faux heroes as they look for new routes
into happiness or truth which is what *he she and I* hoped for that very electric night

with klieg lights strafing the sky and the glamorous town in all our varied minds
rooting for us to enter the garden beneath a fresh version of the pantheon of stars.

ROOTING FOR THE DEAD

When Ben was sixteen his father beckoned with an index finger
and said he had a chore for him to do so they drove silently to

the Institute where his father worked and he was shown how
to grip the bodies of grown rabbits while his nerdy dad axed off

their heads in quick succession so the blood would drain quickly
and the brains would remain clean for study; they killed thirty-six

that way in half an hour then his father took him quietly back
to the softball field to rejoin his friends where the grass was

damp under a cobalt sky after a violent storm but his friends
had turned wooden forever as only fear could contain what was

left of the faith he had always counted on though on good days
it still rises like mist from the ground he roots around even as

the eyes of God cloud and the rabbits he needs scamper away.

JELLY JARS

My grandmother, who was a large woman in a small
apartment by the time I knew her, would squeal when handling
the Flintstone jelly jars she used for serving juice—
she'd fill them up and marvel at the way
some cheerful TV cartoon kept lingering in her home.
Years later, after graduating college,
I stayed with her, and again would get the jelly jars,
taken reverentially from the open shelf in the tiny alcove,
and hear her marvel at the wonders of modernity—
how a character can be fused into glass
that might just be delivering jelly, but for this woman,
given what she'd endured, remained the gift to share with me.

GRACE RETURNS

At 5 A.M. she tiptoes out of her room to the small wooden desk
under the dim light beneath the hotel stairs to find Juan's things:

a jar full of uncooked rice and beans, a drained coffee cup,
a half-eaten *bolillo*, a bag of rags. Juan is the night maid and fills

his buckets, mops till dawn . . . listens to Dylan and Dion on his
transistor radio, their bold lyrics softened by the Spanish tongue.

He nods toward Grace and smiles—touches the back of her hand as
the roof-rooster crows, then speaks, though she does not understand.

He knows that to her, his world appears grim, but trusts
they will share the levitation, this cultivation at the edge of the Indian—

their impulse to sing with the bells of the Parroquia, which will mill
them into the soft bread the Padre later slips between their teeth.

SHE COMES

She passes the refinery, turns left at the mini-mart, descends into the neighborhood where the old house sits in disrepair, enters through the pocked door but soon gets blinded by the smell of loneliness arcing across the bare walls like jism trails before that grind of heroin finding an arm … for there are no toys except guns and one tired broken Game Boy—no clothes or exorcist tools, although change is what she's come for as she hacks at the walls with her own scarred wrists and weeps, or reddens like the picked sores drifting away from her body yet still no answer as the sun descends over All Souls Graveyard next door, its stones rooted to the ground by our still-warm wonder … she comes because of the bad dream he forced upon her with the pills, the strap, with the steady haze over the valley that delivers a stubborn cough, prosthetic limbs and turns this woman into a lantern combing for veins in her dead man's mine.

DESERT

Everywhere light lands on the desert house and even the deserted souls
shut up tightly can feel it seeping in as if their insides slowly coming out

were worth the spotlight; my photographer heads to such god-forsaken
towns amid the groves and sands but mostly sands with brutal heat and

white carports that lodge the souls who keep re-emerging in this desert
where the flimsy walls and blushing roof tiles and a satellite dish bigger

than an old garage loom over spits of pavement and sandy creosote that
remain the best evidence of our angry remembering and last drive-in of

the drug of not knowing—solitude and redemption here where the Lord
called *people of the city* refuse to see the enduring heat of how we suffer.

FOLK-ROCK

The road to Topanga wound through arid crumbling hillsides which advertised
primitive to Willie and Linda from Los Angeles who'd chosen the new forsaking

as the war grew stronger. When they reached the cinematic canyon town with
its odor of wealth stumbling to pious knees for the suck of strange water Linda

became Butterfly and Willie pinned her wings to his dreams of flight then came
out one year later as dark as the storm the earth needs to birth so men can sing.

THE SAD STORY OF US

Gio and Renata drove their Ford to the remote slip on the river
and let the car roll naturally down the concrete ramp and into the water
where it began to sink as they giggled and pawed each other in the back seat
and because time is such a goofball it hatched Gio and Renata's story
before the waters overtook them and they had children and grandchildren
and he threw his back out and she had to work retail and smile at buffoons
while the waters kept rising as the canyon filled with their scent and
then they were gone, just one beam of senseless light from the lonesome sun.

JUST US

Edna and I, we pulled off some great parties in the past—
couples who were going places, and because of Edna's job

the booze was good . . . now, I guess we call it pasture time;
our friends tend to be nurses, or folks who can't quite hear;

the grounds are beautiful; I could almost play golf, if I could;
and the trees at the far edge of the lawn wander—they're

my youth creeping in; but mostly it's the warm tropical air,
the worry balls, the fruit juice, and Edna, who can still plan

a mean party . . . though now it's our memories that dance
and the pride of still being here, and the way her old hand

lifts to her huge breast whenever I say something shocking.

HOW WE LOVE

Walking the path beyond the house
in a fog that was thick and disquieting
Jason slipped off his body and entered
the voice of a greater authority and soon
the fog became just that moistening
of the transcendental eye and he
could feel grief for the plight of everyone
which was less of a beach-house crush
than the ring within which he grew warm
as the summer fields grow warm
as his god flushes with warm while
plumping up the pillows in her bedroom
eager to move through his disquietude.

IV

ON THE FRONTIER

TONIC MINOR

Cycling the north coast I think of the birth of cool
as a blue jay follows me, darting and dipping like Miles.

This sound is not ours alone. The trumpet in the darkened
club, dense with grief, with revelation, rises out of the blood

of all Earth's creatures, out of the light that sinks into every
frantic eye. I know this bird is not sorrow, I know this bird

is not grief, but the dark clouds suckling the hills are almost
the breast that fills the baby—nearly the waves that slow the

backbeat to make the human swoon. I am riding north to
escape this body, to encourage wind in its persistent desire

to change us. I am riding bird and I am alone, like the giant
onstage whose eyes glaze to increase the miles, who welcomes

shocks from the road—a sudden lightning, because birds can
sense when the earth is about to give, its cymbals will hush ...

when the sister mysteries will blow out the final note we love.

QUILT COUNTRY

One morning Jon got up before the others and pulled on his jeans and T-shirt
and those boots that had been everywhere and stepped out into the front yard

which had a small garden of its own and plucked two dark berries then went to
the barn to calm the cows before heading down the road that takes three bends

then enters the five-block town with the single stoplight before plowing back
into the young corn he relishes as the font of imagination but as he walked into

the next state the swifts in the bell tower of the ancient church in the forgotten
country swooped down and began to circle him so he commenced to toll with the

grief of his family and its ghastly hubris and soon pale light drained the horizon
and he could see the outlines of the swifts more clearly as their patterns of flight

passed the filter of his heart for he'd grown suddenly German here on the plains
of America like the Jews did throughout Christendom and before long came

reflexive ways for the souls of men to be like the ripening leaves of late summer
all wet with benediction as their rich green color grows toward the darker days

and now the world graced him with cows and field mice and even those tractors
who have no mind of their own though they were once *hope boundless* as the sky's

pink grew orange briefly then a blue unlike any other except maybe the folds on
the gowns of the Virgin as her Christ-child turns naturally and impetuously away.

BORDER

We walked across the border into the Mexican town crowded with hawkers and
street crud then stepped into the one modern building which housed the museum

my father hoped to show his art in but it was nearly empty save for the desk clerk
and some sculptor in the back room who was also the curator so we were directed

to him and he stepped away from the wire and plaster to usher us into an alcove
with a computer where my father tried to explain in broken Spanish the purpose

of his philosophical statements on whiteboards in both Spanish and English which
tugged the wisdom of the ancients through the solipsistic self and the curator nearly

fifty years younger with a tattoo of the Virgin on one bicep and Jesus on the other
listened politely and nodded then asked *but what about the images?* and my father

who had discovered philosophy in the Kike-Wop section of the Bronx back when
America was digesting itself in order to build a stronger nation said *it's not about*

the images but the way ideas tip the cart full of all of us off a cliff so revelation can
get good tailwind behind it and though he was misrepresenting himself the young

sculptor-curator considered my father's being nicely the way the old Aztecs might
have if Cortez had been more cartoon and less brutality then he said *sí white man*

no he didn't say white man *I will consider it because art means nothing if we're not*
all in this together for I'd been sitting in a chair in the corner contemplating man's

origins and destinations and wished I spoke Spanish but it'd been shelved because
there was so much damage to contain and then we all shook hands and the curator's

was firm and warm and my father's was cooler and fading and thus we ended and
walked out into the chaotic city and soon across the border like those artful Greeks.

JÉSUS

sits in front of the old Engineering Building
on the campus of our famous university—

two classic pillars astride ashen cinereal stone
and supporting the engraved word: *Engineering*

so quaint in its certitude given how narrow the building
when compared to the standard of these end of days . . .

Jésus turns off his computer
and slides it into a backpack stuffed with books

then puts his chin between his knees
and begins to whisper to the land he's come from—

his family's loyal racketeering
its dark center of magnificent configuration

and soon—as in all great religion—the words widen
to swell with the dignity and power

of men resuming their rightful proportion
and for a time the heavy machinery returns to its shed

and the hologram he mistook for truth
retreats at the dip of a finger

and when Jésus lifts his head via lips still wet
with kisses the pillars rebound

and the Word rebuilds before his eyes
as *Tend* reengineered for this land of the replaced.

TRANSMISSION

When I introduced C. K. Williams at a benefit for *Columbia: A Magazine of Poetry and Prose* in 1984 because I was the poetry editor and thus the emcee I ladled on the irony even in my short introduction and he critiqued me wryly after he took the stage saying he had never been introduced like *that* before then proceeded to read poems he had just published in *Tar* about adolescent boys visiting whores or pelting dead deer snagged by river rocks . . . or standing transfixed by the magazines in some destitute Pennsylvania town which showed brutal men fisting; now in the year of his death the old tears come as I try to remind him that irony is how we love.

THE BICYCLE

for Paul Zweig

The man who taught us Whitman rode his bike through the streets of New York,
long before fashionable, to get to our fancy university
where he kept professing Walt's "too-muchness" as he deconstructed
the long loping sentences one after another,
and though he'd published his fine biography of the poet and we were the elite,
nothing spoke up like that bicycle, chained to its pole outside Dodge Hall,
where the brakes and the bald tires waited patiently for their necessary man
to come back again, but then suddenly he died, taken by a swift and virulent cancer,
so I returned to the way I had first learned Whitman—reading his poems
as I walked the streets of another coast, intuiting curbs and lampposts and cars
and whistling for my unleashed dog without looking up,
for the words kept erupting like liberated spoons with the perfect medicine,
and I became an angel, which is how and when we realize we will die, for no city,
nor the daft can take the transcendent wisdom of a swift and simple vehicle away.

REBUTTAL

after Robert Frost

When I was a boy to climb a tree
was the easiest way to unhook from sorrow—
the firm feel of wood to lean upon
and leverage for some greater height
as one goes up was sweeter
than what I'd found on common ground
searching among fallen fruits and nuts
for something that would get me so I could eat.
The sky was an inkling of some greater park
with fantastic swings and deeper pools
as the branches thinned and the wind revived.
The thrill of going higher was closer to *truth*
than some classroom where boys and girls played
like cheap toys and broke if handled ardently.
I preferred ardent about the sky,
and thus am here alone, just below timberline,
still climbing, my old friends like
branches suspending me as I head for heaven
which is the best place for love.

CAMDEN

for Edna

On the coast of Maine
where the flushed sun
touches first I flush
beneath hard maples
and quiet elms alive in
the victory of being
akin to the poet stringing
her hammock and
pounding the book which
like a beam clearing
the dark in skulls signals
home to our sailors
as they struggle in from
the youth of man.

THOSE OTHER BOYS

In the days and weeks following the 9/11 attacks
I began to look differently at the rough boys,
with their tattoos and trucks and their snarling reflexive patriotism.
Previously the enemy, they were at least on *our* side,
and eager to charge into the breach, so comfortable with violence,
for *dark* was still beyond them, but encroaching, though it did not speak.
Or rather, not in a language they could understand.
Now it's ten years on, and again I'm suspicious,
when the foreign radiates with visceral knowledge, but I drink from it,
as my skin withers and the joints ache and the dark comes closer.

THE CITY COMES

At the corner of White Street and some darker boulevard
the old heart keeps thudding like an ax far outside the body
for it responds to the touch of the myth that infills the city
the way the zealot's blood infills each of us on our target days
which is why when strangers pass they see only the naked organ
insolent in its exit from the way things should be
but those of us who know the hysterical ventricles
and the spray of feeling when sin is true to one's history
can confirm there is no greater spectacle than the doubt inside
this determination to rework the intersection for the city is where
we lie quietly vulnerable and pulsing for what we trust it will give.

FLAT ARROW

One Penn Plaza rises sleek and dark and angular
over what used to be arced and light and ornate

and the sorrow inside the power of this is what
we might remember about the modern impulse

as the earth disgorges men for building wildly...
for while we aim hard not to be wrong we are

limited inside our powerful tools by the sweet
distance that remains between this and heaven.

A NEW MUSEUM

Berkeley, 2016

Begin with the idea that nations might get along
which means people regardless of chinks or error

and add art which is faith in the perfect expression
then drape it like mercury over the old masonry home

where the Charter was run so men could keep believing
in what was squeezed from the ruins of the worst of wars

and marry one's reason to serendipity which is an instinct
like hate or love to let the gist of the true university shine on

its western hinge while ideas turned into life keep flourishing
like some paradise the beam of art was always torqued to build.

GRIEF

Tom drives up from Memorial Valley
and when he arrives at the base of the ridge
the high pines wander down to greet him
for they understand how
a man can exit his body to pollinate the trees
and mix with sap and immigrant blood
until *pine* becomes something we do
for those who came before
but were so deformed by scorching heat
and brutal winds they longed for the valley
and complained they had seen enough of heights
though it is those heights that set us free.

FOR NADINE, WHO IS STILL WITH US

When you reached up through the veil of hospital gasses
to the women who came to welcome you into the grotto
where the cooling mist eased the first phase of the transition
I could see in the way you took your last breath
all winnowed and expectant like the chosen one
that breath had simply been training for suspiration of
a different kind so the crown of heaven can become a second skin.

I think of you still with your wings outspread and shedding
wisps of us yet going nowhere for that's the way you did things
waiting for your friends to join even though the gates were closing
although knowing and loving you filled one with the knowledge
that no gates were closing just simply breathing as the rest of us
press onward unconscious through this conduit of flesh.

FOR MARY

In Bologna my wife studies a menu at a street-side café looking as lovely and
self-possessed as the swifts circling the nave of the sixth century church while
medieval organs groan because we are in the city of the West's oldest university
and inquisitive nature is a minyan including mine now watching us age and
grow more beautiful with time as the stone and tile and the stained glass do
in this home of the young where Mozart came at fourteen as did so many others
I could name if only I had loved them half as much as I love this woman and the
birds circling as the rings of fragrance rise and seek their dissolution into heaven.

TASSAJARA

I meditate on the large rock in the middle of the stream
and follow my breath while listening to the current
which reminds me everything that passes   has passed before

and my limbs are folded and inert in the warm breeze
for the body is a trickster or rather some faux-inverse of water
and I know I should be delighted   so I am

yet have a stone in my heart as heavy as the ravaged planet
for the body is not inert but a peel of light escaped from death
alive and well wherever our brio is blooming

and all that's good and all that's horrible is reconvened
while I sit molting here where human eyes can't see me
for they are over on the bank with their toes in baffled water

along with crackers and wine which connect them
to the greater body the way the wolf howl is the animal
loving not me but what loves me   or rather the dream of me

and Jane is in the middle of the stream not molting nor shelled
but gamely recollecting what is real for she's the one who'll read
this poem which is sometimes the only way she touches stone.

STUDY

I return to the creek out back of Philosophy Hall
with weaker eyesight and rafts of regret and irritation
            which float past endlessly

but water still spills over the rocks
as it did the first time
and the green looks sumptuous in the light

and in the shade too where the grief that produced
wisdom still heaves
            I read Emerson   only now it's more like

bidding him adieu than
sucking from his words a marrow for these bones
but maybe not

maybe it's more like *hold on*
while I do those things I still yearn to
like die   pursue glory   or both

it was a good philosophy of life
I found here years ago
escaping into the urban woodlands

where trees live like sensuous refugees
and water will not be denied
and the sunlight through which we grow
                forks in

like the pale-green building across the stream
gothic-arched with tiny leadened windows
from which there's still so much to be seen.

Sixteen Rivers Press is a shared-work, nonprofit poetry collective
dedicated to providing an alternative publishing avenue for
Northern California poets. Founded in 1999 by seven writers,
the press is named for the sixteen rivers
that flow into San Francisco Bay.

SAN JOAQUIN • FRESNO • CHOWCHILLA • MERCED • TUOLUMNE

STANISLAUS • CALAVERAS • BEAR • MOKELUMNE • COSUMNES • AMERICAN

YUBA • FEATHER • SACRAMENTO • NAPA • PETALUMA